Walks Around
STOURBRIDGE

by Stourbridge Group -
Ramblers' Association
edited by John Roberts

****

WALKWAYS
J S Roberts
8 Hillside Close, Bartley Green
Birmingham B32 4LT

****

Walks around
Stourbridge

by Stourbridge Group - Ramblers' Association
edited by John Roberts

ISBN 0 947708 35 9

First Published 1997

Meet the Group

The Stourbridge Group of the Ramblers' Association was formed in 1982. It has grown into a friendly and dynamic body which is going from strength to strength.

We organise some 40 walks each year, and most start at 10.00 am on Sundays and range from 5 to 10 miles. We explore all the local areas of Worcestershire, Warwickshire Staffordshire and Shropshire, and sometimes go further with holidays in Wales. Our many social events include dinners, visits and social evenings.

A primary aim of the Ramblers' Association is to protect public footpaths, bridleways and green lanes, and in our Group's territory there are many. We have friendly relations with local farmers and our stiles team makes repairs, erects marker posts and clears undergrowth. Problems met elsewhere are reported to the local council. We also comment on diversion proposals or other developments which might affect paths, sometimes agreeing, sometimes objecting.

Walking is Britain's most popular pastime. This is recognised by the Countryside Commission who have set local Councils the target of getting all the paths in their areas clearly marked and unobstructed by the year 2000. We are doing our best to make sure the target is met.

In 1995 the Ramblers' Association celebrated its Jubilee Year - 60 years of working for walkers. This book is the Stourbridge Group's contribution and marks our own 15th birthday. Enjoy these local walks, celebrate with us and help the Countryside Commission to hit the target. Most of them can be reached by bus and a few by train, but if you go by car we have made sure there is somewhere to park. The walking is easy, pleasant and interesting, and will give you a real taste of what the group can offer.

Many thanks to all members of the group who helped in any way with this book, by contributing walks, writing or testing them or by distributing it. Thanks in particular to John Roberts without whose help it would not have been possible.

We hope that you will enjoy these walks, and if you would like more in good company, the Group will give you a warm welcome. You can see a copy of our programme at local Libraries and can reach us through RA's Central Office at 1/5 Wandsworth Road London, SW8 2XX (0171 582 6878), or by phoning John Roberts on 0121 550 3158.

John Allen
Chairman
May 1997

Contents

Our Local Landscape

The walks in this book lead you along ancient. sandy tracks. canal towpaths and fieldpaths to visit secret ponds, sandstone cliffs, brackeny hills and rustling woods - and all near Stourbridge.

Stourbridge was a market town once centred on Old Swinford but long years ago moved away towards the River Stour. As the community developed it was served not only by roads heading for the "bridge", but by canal and railway. The Stour rises on the Clent Hills and runs through Halesowen and the Black Country before escaping through Stourbridge to green fields. Industrial pollution is much reduced, but it is a hard worked little river and by no means clean.

Stourbridge sits on the south-west corner of the West Midland area and is traditionally and physically part of the Black Country. In earlier times its river drove water mills to grind corn and make iron and steel tools. Flint and cut glass making was introduced from Lorraine. The firm of Foster Rastrick built steam locomotives, of which the most famous was *Agenoria* for the Earl of Dudley's railway at Shut End. Another was the *Lion*, which in 1829 was the first locomotive to run in America.

In its main streets and older buildings Stourbridge still has something of the market town; the Talbot in the High Street was obviously a coaching inn, the genial brick and stone St Thomas's church of 1728 might serve a country parish. Even though these last two hundred years of our town's history has been industrial, it is crowded on three sides by fine countryside treasured by Stourbridge and Black Country people. It was recently announced that the planned Western Orbital Motorway between Bromsgrove and Wolverhampton had been abandoned. This monster would have ravaged the landscape, so you can imagine our relief.

West of the town is a broad belt of undulating, sandy ground, and from the north the Smestow Brook winds through it to meet the Stour, which then appropriates its valley and continues south to the River Severn. Beyond the rivers are blocks of higher ground, the Sheepwalks and Kinver Edge. These sandstone outcrops are the first in a series of ridges and valleys which roll west to the Severn, growing as they cross Shropshire. The Edge is a richly wooded, two mile bluff from which you can see the Clee Hills, Abberley Hills and the Malverns, and of course the nearby Clent Hills.

South of Stourbridge the ground is still sandy but more level, except for the steep and rounded Clent Hills. They mark two points. Some of the views on these walks show that much of the conurbation is on hilly ground. The Clent Hills mark a western rampart of this area and the edge of the so called Birmingham Plateau. To the south the ground falls gradually into the Severn Plain. The Clent Hills are composed of broken, shaley rock with main peaks in Adams Hill and Walton Hill. They are steep and bald and grassy with woodland on the lower flanks.

The past and present of Black Country industry and rural traditions mingle in this landscape. Kinver Edge and the Clents have seen generations of Black Country workers on holiday. The Edge once formed part of a Royal Forest some eighteen miles long and fifteen wide which in 1688 turned over to farming. Kinver still has a village atmosphere and a good supply of cafes and pubs. Clent village is much smaller and has no real centre. It lay in the Royal Forest of Feckenham and its name is still spelt as in the Domesday Book. Pretty Belbroughton has a real babbling brook which once powered mills to make scythes, while sedate Blakedown went in for spades and shovels.

Walking is our natural pace in the countryside; you can see and hear it, smell the air and feel the breeze. Happy walking and rich memories.

The Country Code

* Enjoy the countryside and respect its life and work
* Guard against all risk of fire
* Fasten all gates
* Keep your dogs under close control
* Keep to public paths across farmland
* Use gates and stiles to cross fences, hedges and walls
* Leave livestock, crops and machinery alone
* Take your litter home
* Help to keep water clean
* Protect wildlife, plants and trees
* Take special care on country roads
* Make no unnecessary noise

Boots & Clothes & Things

These walks are all modest affairs so you do not need to go equipped for mountaineering. However, a few simple things will do a great deal to keep you comfortable and so enjoy your walks, which is what we want. Here are some hints.

These walks can be muddy in wet weather. Walking boots are best, but for short walks wear wellies if you find them comfortable. Trainers are excellent in dry weather. Good woolly socks are a great comfort. The traditional grey, rough wool ragsock is thick and hardwearing, but that is about all. Try loop pile socks. Apart from suitable footwear the other greatest contributors to comfort are a hat, a waterproof with a hood, and gloves.

If you enjoy these walks and want to take up walking as a pastime, there are many books and shops that offer sound advice on boots, clothing and equipment.

Rights of Way & Obstructions

These walks are all on public Rights of Way, which may be Footpaths, Bridleways or Byways (usually green lanes or tracks) with some sections of ordinary road. Your rights as pedestrian are the same on all, you may follow the track or cross the land. That land is "private" is irrelevant.

It is a criminal offence to obstruct these ways, for example by ploughing paths without reinstating them or sowing crops over them. You may cross or remove such obstacles doing as little damage as you reasonably can. You may diverge to pass the obstacle so long as you go no further than necessary and do not enter anyone else's land.

These notes appear in all WALKWAYS books but you are not likely to meet any problems on these walks. If you do please contact the publisher.

Amendment Service

The countryside changes all the time. You could meet new tracks, stiles and barns; hedges vanish and paths may be diverted. To keep directions as up to date as possible WALKWAYS issues amendment slips.

IF you write to tell of any changes or problems that you meet, stating route and paragraph number, they will refund your postage.

IF you send a stamped addressed envelope with a note of what books you have, they will send you up to date amendment slips. (Telephone enquiries welcome - 0121 550 3158)

Using the Directions

The walking directions are separate from description and comment, quite terse, and set in short, numbered paragraphs in a clear and open typeface. These and less obvious features have been adopted for Walkways books after much thought and experience. They aim to give information in easily found and remembered blocks of convenient size, bearing in mind that you will be reading them on the move.

Distances in *yards* or *miles* are to give you a ROUGH idea how far to walk. You do not need to measure because you will be given something to look out for, such as a stile or the old mill. If we say "go 1/2 mile", you will not start to worry if you cannot see the old mill, or whatever, after 200 yards. We use yards where you will know how far we mean, but few people know what 600 yards looks like, so for longer distances we turn to fractions of a mile.

Distances in *paces* are given to be counted out if you need to. These are infrequent and only for a few yards at a time. Paces vary but you can allow for being tall or short. People carry a pace with them, but not usually a measuring tape.

We have largely avoided abbreviations but certain phrases recur. You will sometimes see *half R* (or L) meaning a half turn, or about 45 degrees. Therefore *bear R* (or L) means a narrower angle than a half turn, or just tending away from straight ahead. A *road* has a tarmac surface and is usually big enough for a white line down the middle. *Lanes* are tarmaced but smaller. *Drives* are like lanes but not public. *Tracks* are wide enough for a four wheeled vehicle, even a small one; they may have an earth, grass or stone surface. A *path* may have any surface, from mud to tarmac, but is only pedestrian width.

The maps are sketches to an approximate scale of 2 1/2 ins /1 mile (4cms/1km), and designed to confirm where you are rather than for route finding. The big black arrow on each map points to north, but you had guessed as much, hadn't you? The meanings of the symbols are mainly obvious but we show a few of them below. The numbers of some paragraphs from the route descriptions appear on the maps.

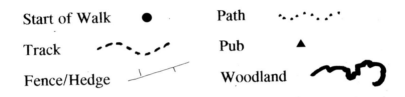

From our directions and maps you should find your way very well, but many people like to carry Ordnance Survey maps. They will help you find starting points more easily, and might be useful in case you want to leave the route for an urgent haircut, or something. For each village we note the numbers of the OS Landranger (1:50,000 - 1 1/4ins/1 mile or 2cms/1 km) and the more detailed Pathfinder (1: 25,000 - 2 1/2ins/1 mile or 4cms/1 km).

Getting to the Start

These walks have been carefully devised so that the starting points are easy to reach and to recognise. With each walk we give advice on getting there by bus, train and car, and on parking.

BUSES AND TRAINS
Services change, so the best we can do is tell you in each case whether there was a service when we visited. We also note the enquiry phones so you can get up to date details.

CARS

We have made sure that there are suitable places for a few cars near starting points. Please use a car park if there is one and take great care never to cause any obstruction or inconvenience. Do not use pub car parks without permission. However, we have never met a landlord who was not happy for you to leave your car if you intend to finish your walk with a drink or a meal. It isn't a bad idea anyway.

List of Walks

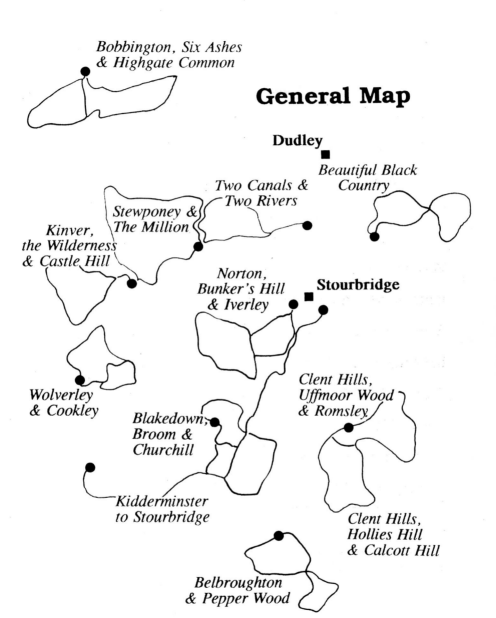

Bobbington, Six Ashes & Highgate Common

General Map

Dudley

Beautiful Black Country

Two Canals & Two Rivers

Stewponey & The Million

Kinver, the Wilderness & Castle Hill

Norton, Bunker's Hill & Iverley

Stourbridge

Wolverley & Cookley

Blakedown, Broom & Churchill

Clent Hills, Uffmoor Wood & Romsley

Kidderminster to Stourbridge

Clent Hills, Hollies Hill & Calcott Hill

Belbroughton & Pepper Wood

Beautiful Black Country

WHERE
Start from Saltwells Wood east from the A4036 Lye - Dudley
road and the south entrance to the Merry Hill Centre; map
reference SO 934869. Maps: Landranger Birmingham 139,
Pathfinder 933 SO 88/98.

TRANSPORT, PARK & START
Buses pass; enquiries 0121 200 2700. Park in the area prov-
ided; the walk starts here.

REFRESHMENTS
The Saltwells Inn (Banks's) at the start, and on the way you
meet the Hope Tavern (Banks's), White Swan (Pubmaster),
The Hailstone (Hanson's) and the Dry Dock (Little Pub).

HOW FAR
7 miles or a short walk of 4 1/2 miles.

A WOOD, CANALS, A MOUNTAIN AND A HOLE
This fascinating walk has beautiful woodland, a lake,
canals, a modest mountain, a vast crater and spectacular
views, but it will not be to everyone's taste. The circuit
explores some inner parts of the Black Country and is
frankly industrial. Even so, it leads you for seven miles
using no more than 500 yards of urban road, because
this hard worked area has many green spaces linked by
canals and old railway tracks.

The walk starts and ends in the 100 acre Saltwells Wood.
From the early 18th century the area was mined for coal
and from 1870 to 1945, for clay. The woodland near the
claypit is what remains of trees planted in the mid 18th
century to cover the scars. Other old trees are survivors
of Pensnett Chase. The main species is oak, with birch
and holly. In the valleys are beech, ash, lime, poplar
and sycamore.

The walk passes the tree fringed Lodge Farm Reservoir which serves the Dudley No 2 Canal. This opened in 1797 and runs from the mouth of the narrow and sagging Dudley Tunnel round Netherton Hill to the wider Netherton Tunnel. The walk crosses its mouth, and you can walk through if you fancy nearly two miles of cold, damp darkness. Nearby is Cobb's Engine House with its lofty, iron bound brick chimney. The engine once pumped water from local mines and is now in the Henry Ford Museum at Dearborn, USA, and they are not minded to return it.

The walk meets two hills. Netherton Hill at 189 metres is a smooth dome crowned by a church; a strange, abandoned place covered in a straggle of gorse and coarse grass. The high point of the walk is Rough Hill at 260 metres, which rears abruptly out of the tumbling valleys of factories and houses. The distant views include all hills visible from the Clent Hills whilst beneath is a huge industrial panorama which Lowry could not have imagined.

(1) From car park, take track past house & pub L to cross stile by gate. Go on 150yds to 5 track junction.

(2) Go R, pass path R, & continue 300yds to junction of tracks with field ahead.

(3) Go R by field to junction, then turn L up to gate. DON'T TAKE IT. Turn R up steps & follow path to T junction. Go L (past side paths) up to gate & road.

(4) Go R up steps to tarmac drive & turn R by reservoir. Curve L to yacht club, then follow its fence round to join path by canal.

(5) Follow canal 1/2 mile (under brick bridge) to two iron bridges. Fork L past footbridge & circle round to cross Cattle Bridge.

(6) Meet track, go L 1/4 mile & cross stile to lane.

(7) Go R 250yds past 1st gate L to 2nd, & take kissing gate.

(8) Follow path past R fork & steps L, then follow fence to its end. Go down L, then curve R up to gate & road.

(9) Cross road, go R 150yds to Hope Tavern, & take Swan Street L. Follow it to White Swan & T junction.

(10) Cross road, go L 50yds to opposite Round Street & take gap R. Cross playground & climb steps.

(11) Go ahead, bearing R to join footway. Follow it to blue bridge & take tunnel.

(12) Follow woodland path & cross a path. Keep this line 300yds & pass 1st phone pole to 2nd. Take track L & cross canal.

****
SHORT WALK
Go R to canal junction, then switch to
para (21).
****

(13) Go L past chimney & take green track ahead with pool R. Follow it up to open grass area. Go ahead to road, bearing L to join it at blue brick ventilation tower.

(14) Cross stile opposite & follow path, curving R to path junction. Go ahead between bushes (past path R) to join fenced track.

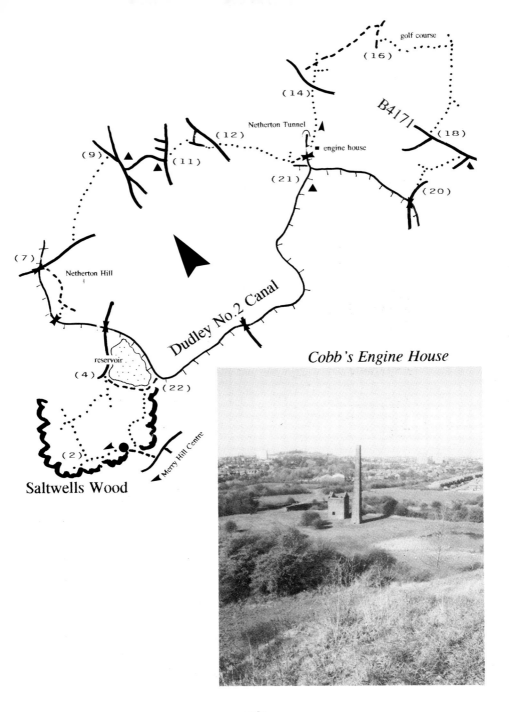

golf course

(16)

(14)

Netherton Tunnel

B4171

(18)

engine house

(12)

(9)

(11)

(21)

(20)

(7)

Netherton Hill

Dudley No.2 Canal

Cobb's Engine House

reservoir

(4)

(22)

(2)

Merry Hill Centre

Saltwells Wood

(15) Follow it up to end of R fence, then take track R up to level track. Go R 50yds to pole. Turn L on small grass path to open area.

(16) Bear R towards golf club's marker pole & meet cliff. Go R & follow grass path beside it past fence post to tree in path. Go ahead on LEVEL path round edge of course, till it ends on course. Head for NEAREST pine clump & meet track.

(17) Go down R & cross stile. Follow R hedge/fence (via middle stile) to cross bottom stile. Go ahead on fenced path to road.

(18) Cross & go L 80yds to Post Office. Turn R down Springfield Close to its end, then down L on tarmac path.

(19) Follow to R bend, then fork L till path ends at brick wall. Go R, cross end of road & take path to road.

(20) Cross, go R & over canal, then turn L onto towpath. GO UNDER BRIDGE & walk 1/4 mile to canal junction.

(21) Go L ("Stourbridge") & follow canal 1 1/4 miles. After Saltwells Bridge watch for yacht club, & fork L from canal.

(22) Cross turning area to join track, & before 1st house, cross stile L. Go down by R fence to junction then turn R & follow fence to its end. Bear R & pass paths R to start.

Belbroughton & Pepper Wood

WHERE
A village on the B4188 just off the A491 and 5 miles south-
east of Stourbridge. Maps: Landranger 139, Pathfinder 953
SO 87/97. Map reference SO 919769.

TRANSPORT, PARK & START
Buses call; enquiries 01905 763763. Park opposite the church
from where the walk starts.

REFRESHMENTS
The Talbot (Hansons), The Old Mill (Free House), and The
Queens (Marston's).

HOW FAR
7 1/2 miles or a short walk of 4 1/4 miles.

FIELDS, HILLS, SCYTHES & A WOOD
Fieldpaths and tracks lead over small, round hills, through
a wood and past a bright pool. This rolling landscape gives
up new secrets and views with every rise and fold.

Belbroughton is hilly with a mixture of timber framed, 18th
and 19th century brick and modern houses. In the 16th century a mill powered by the Belne Brook made sword blades,
and by the 18th century the brook was driving five corn mills
and scythe making forges. In the 19th century scythes were
exported worldwide, but the market declined and the works
closed in 1967. You can find old millstones in garden walls,
steps and weirs. A plating hammer stands on the village
green.

Holy Trinity church has Norman doorways and a south window
but is mainly 19th century. The chancel arch shows vague red
patches which are fragmants of wall paintings. A 17th century
pulpit is carved with dragons and weird human figures.

(1) From church lychgate, go up to near school & turn L on tarmac path. Follow past gardens to tarmac drive by tennis courts.

(2) Go R past building & follow R hedge (via 2 stiles) to open field. Bear R to double power pole & cross stile.

(3) Go ahead to stone wall, follow its R side to rear & bear L to cross stile. Follow sunken path to cross stile, then follow R hedge up to take small gate.

(4) Go ahead with trees on your R, then hedge on your L & through hedge gap. Follow midfield track up to white farm & cross stile L.

(5) Bear R through gate, cross yard & take gate onto track.

****
SHORT WALK
switch to para (17)
****

(6) Take steel gate L & go L up field edge track to take top gateway. Go R 50yds, then half L through orchard to its corner, & cross stile.

(7) Go L by hedge to corner, pass pond on your R & go through thicket to field. Follow L hedge & take corner gap. Go L, round field corner & down to bottom corner. Go R by hedge 250yds & turn L by railings.

(8) Follow woodland path through dingle & up to gate. DON'T TAKE IT. Go R by fence, continue through wood to gate, & cross stile.

(9) Go R by fence up to ruin and cross stile. Go ahead & down to cross hedgerow. Follow wood edge 100yds to markpost & take path R.

(10) Go down to cross footbridge then up to stile & field. Go ahead by wood 100yds to big oak, & cross stile R. Go L by fence, past gate L, & cross stile to lane.

(11) Go R 1/4 mile (lane becomes track), to steel gate with barn R. Turn L down stone track (past track R) to car park & road

(12) Take track opposite to pass between buildings & take gateway to field. Follow L hedge & take next gate.

(13) Go R by hedge to field corner & cross stile. Go ahead to cross midhedge stile. Follow L FENCE past gate to stile & road.

(14) Go R 100yds & cross stile L. Go half R to cross MIDHEDGE STILE. Follow R hedge (via 2 fields) to bottom of 3rd, then cross concrete bridge & take gate R.

(15) Bear L up to gate fronting L of 2 red brick houses, & cross stile to lane. Go R 350 yds to pass Poolhouse Farm, & cross stile R.

(16) Go half L & cross twin stiles. Go half L to R end of black barn & take steel gate onto track.

(17) Follow track to road. Go R (past track R) 300yds, & just pass farm gate L cross stile L.

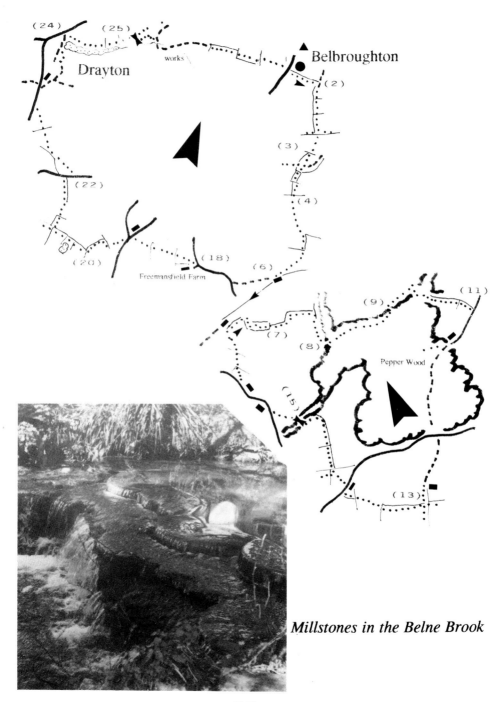

(24)   (25)   works   Belbroughton
Drayton   (2)

(3)

(22)   (4)

(20)   (18)   (6)
Freemansfield Farm

(9)   (11)

(7)   (8)   Pepper Wood

(13)

Millstones in the Belne Brook

(17)

(18) Go ahead, bearing R from barns & down to take 1st gate. Go ahead & cross midhedge stile. Head for white house & cross stile to road.

(19) Go L to road junction, then bear R & take fenced path between bungalows to field. Go R, follow hedge round 2 corners & join sunken path to cross stile.

(20) Go ahead & cross 2 stiles by pond, then bear R to field corner & cross stile. Go ahead 10yds & cross stile R.

(21) Follow L hedge & cross stile. Keep same line ahead to end of hedge, then with hedge on your R to gate/stile & lane.

(22) Cross stile opposite. Bear L & cross summit, & keep same line (via midhedge gate) to field corner, & cross stile to lane.

(23) Go R to house & take track R. Pass track R & follow brick drive past houses, then join green track to end. Take small gate & follow R fence down to track. Go R to bend of road.

(24) Go R over stile & follow pool, then stream, for 1/2 mile, & cross footbridge R.

(25) Go L & follow wall to its end, then bear R to track junction. Cross end of track R onto main track. Go R & round sharp L bend, pass works & cross stile.

(26) Go ahead by L hedge & take corner gate. Follow R hedge towards corner, bearing L to enter hedge gap. Follow hedged path to church & pass it on your L back to start.

Blakedown, Broom & Churchill

WHERE
Blakedown is on the A456 Birmingham - Kidderminster road about 4 miles south of Stourbridge. Maps: Landranger 139, Pathfinder 953 SO 87/97. Map reference SO 881786.

TRANSPORT, PARK & START
There are trains and buses; enquiries 0121 643 2711 and 0121 200 2700 respectively. Park at or near the ralway station and start from there.

REFRESHMENTS
The Old House at Home (Ansells) and The Swan (Banks's).

HOW FAR
7 1/2 miles or a short walk of 4 1/4.

POOLS, VALLEYS & SANDY TRACKS
After crossing a slight rise this walk falls into a long, green valley to the hamlet of Hillpool. A gentle climb returns you to higher ground near Broom and Churchill. These small rises and folds of landscape hold a range of farming systems, from sheep pasture to root veg.

Blakedown is brutally cut by the A456 road and for years has suffered speeding traffic and noise. In spite of this, and becoming a dormitory suburb, it stills looks rural and has somehow kept its soul. Recently built traffic calming measures seem to have been fairly sucessful in securing a 30 mph speed limit. The road was once a saltway from Droitwich to the north, and was later improved by the Romans. In 1777 it became a turnpike with a toll house at the junction with the Belbroughton road.

You meet pools as you leave the village, and for a sandy district there seems an awful lot of water about.

There are more waterside alder trees than on the rest of these walks put together. The streams all rise on the Clent Hills, and being fast flowing and reliable, they were dammed at frequent intervals to power water mills for corn and metal working. The highlight of the walk is certainly the narrow and secret valley of the Belne Brook which chases from one side of it to the other, cressy and clear.

The walk skirts the tiny village of Broom, but it is very attractive and worth a visit for its pond and flowery verges. St Peter's is a small, red brick 18th century church.

(1) From station head for A456, but after 50yds go R on track to A456. CARE - go L to cross at lights, then return to pub & take Forge Lane.

(2) Follow to its end & go L onto playing field. Head for far R corner & exit to path. Follow to path T junction.
NEXT - para (3)

****
SHORT WALK
(2a) Go L on fenced path 300yds to B4188. Turn R 1/4 mile to pass house No.91 ("Emohym"!), & take next track L.

(2b) Go 100yds & fork R. Follow woodland path onto field edge, then on 150 yds to wide gap R

(2c) Go L across field to white house.
NEXT - para (18)
****

(3) Go R to far corner of pool. Bear L to join R fence, & follow it on path to lane.

Ladies Pool, Blakedown

(4) Go L 100yds & take track R. Follow it past wood & down to cross stile.

(5) Follow L fence to cross stile, then bear R & cross stile into wood. Go ahead & cross footbridge, then bear L up to field.

(6) Go L 1/4 mile to join track on bend. Go ahead to pass ruin & bend L into dingle. Follow woodland path then sunken track to lane

(7) Go R 1/4 mile to A450. DON'T CROSS YET.

(8) Go R on verge 100yds to phone pole & take gateway opposite. Cross stile, follow R hedge 300yds (via stile), & join path to cross footbridge.

(9) Follow line of stream R (via stiles) 1/2 mile to cross footbridge. Follow wooded path up to lane.

(10) Go R 20 paces & take track L by white railings. Pass gateway on your R & take rising green path L to cross stile. Turn R & cross stile.

(11) Go L by fence to its corner, then keep same line & cross stile ahead to open field. Go ahead midfield to projecting hedge corner. Go ahead with hedge on your L (via hedge gap) to stile & lane.

(12) Take 2nd gate from L ahead. Turn left & follow hedge, joining stone track to T junction. Cross stile opposite & follow L hedge (via stiles) to drive by cottage.

(13) Go R a few paces & enter hedge hole L. Cross footbridge & climb steps to stile & field. Go ahead midfield to midhedge stile & climb steps to road.

(14) Cross stile opposite. Go ahead, bearing slightly L (to TALLEST tree), & cross stile. Go ahead bearing slightly R (ignore stile in R hedge) to field corner, & take gateway.

(15) Go ahead by R fence (via stiles) to lane. Go L to junction, then ahead past church to next junction.

(16) Go L 200yds & pass track L, to cross plank & stile. Go half R & (when in view) head for 40mph sign, & cross stile to A450.

(17) Cross & go L a few paces to take gateway R. Follow track past wood L & through next wood to field edge. Go ahead to white house.

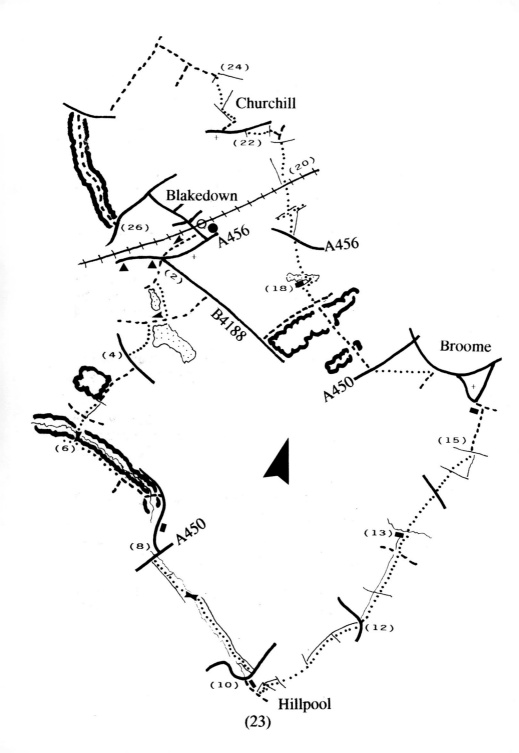

Churchill

(24)

(22)

(20)

Blakedown

(26) A456

A456

(2)

B4188

(18)

Broome

A450

(4)

(15)

(6)

(13)

A450

(8)

(12)

(10)

Hillpool

(23)

(18) Turn R 25 paces & take path down L. Cross dam & climb bank to field edge. Bear slightly L & pass just L of summit of field heading for LONE tree, & cross stile to A456. GREAT CARE.

(19) Cross, go L 30 paces & enter gap R. Follow R hedge towards field corner, then bear L to end of hedge & meet track. Go ahead midfield & cross railway. CARE.

(20) Go half R passing midfield oak on your R to wooden house, & take gate to track.

(21) Go ahead a few paces & take track L to its end. Join hedged path to gate & field. Go ahead following stream R to field corner, & cross stile onto road.

(22) Go L to church & take tarmac drive opposite. Pass 2 entrances L, join green track to gate & cross stile.

(23) Go L by hedge to its corner, then on to cross midhedge stile. Go half R over SUMMIT to far R field corner, & cross stile to hedged track.

(24) Follow 1/4 mile (past track L) to T junction. Go L 1/2 mile to road.

(25) Go R 250yds to far edge of trees & take track L. Follow 1/2 mile to road.

(26) Cross & go L 300yds [R KERB IS SAFEST] to junction, & take road R. Go 1/4 mile to start.

Bobbington, Six Ashes & Highgate Common

WHERE
A small village 2 1/2 miles north-west of Six Ashes on the A458 Stourbridge - Bridgnorth road. Maps: Landranger 138; Pathfinders 912 SO 89/99, 933 SO 88/98 and 932 SO 68/78. Map reference SO 809905.

TRANSPORT, PARK & START
Buses; no effective service. Start from the Red Lion where we have permission to park, but let the landlord know. If the pub is shut put a note in your windscreen.

REFRESHMENTS
Red Lion (Free House), The Six Ashes (Banks's), and Six Ashes Tea Shop & Restaurant.

HOW FAR
8 miles with a short option of 4 1/4 miles.

THREE LANDSCAPES
This walk visits three landscapes. The northern part crosses level fields which are mainly arable and fenced with few hedgerow trees. To the south there is more hedged and hilly grassland, with good tree cover and views of The Sheepwalks, The Million and Kinver Edge. The eastern end of the walk leads through the lowland heath of Highgate Common.

The 278 acres of Highgate Common, with Cannock Chase, the Habberley Valley near Kidderminster and Hartlebury Common at Stourport are the only lowland heaths in the west Midlands. The ground is sandy and dry, forming thin, acid soils. During World War II Highgate was cleared of trees and farmed, after a fashion. But this was a pressure necessity, and after 1949 it reverted to heath. It is now clothed with bilberry, heathers, bracken, and wavy hair grass. Most of the trees are birch, but there is some beech and Corsican pine. On the north side are oaks swathed in wild honeysuckle.

Bobbington has only 500 people living in mainly modern houses, but its name appeared in the Domesday Book. Since the 1950s the village has become a commuter dormitory for Wolverhampton and Dudley. Holy Cross church was dedicated to St Mary until 1905. The first church was Saxon but all that remains of it are the bases of two pillars, and some Norman arches.

[NB abreviation: SW = Staffs Way signs]
(1) Face front of Red Lion, go L 150yds to post box & take drive L. Follow to L bend & join grass track. Keep same line by L hedge & take gateway to open field.

(2) Go ahead to 30yds L of double power pole, & cross stile by gate. Cross 2nd stile (R), then follow R hedge round bend to field corner, & cross plank.

(3) Cross stile by steel post, follow R fence 100yds & cross stile R. Go L 25 paces till fence bends L, then keep ahead into neck of field, & in R corner cross stile. Follow L fence & cross stile to road. CAREFUL.

(4) CROSS HERE & go L 300yds (past drive L & house R) to cross end of 1st track R & take 2nd by signboard.

(5) Follow into field, then follow L hedge to far corner of buildings. Go ahead midfield & take hedge gap, bear L & take midhedge gate.

(6) Cross earth track & take stile. Follow R hedge 400yds; as it bends L WATCH for stiles R, & cross.

(7) Go L to field corner & take gate. Go R by hedge & cross corner stile (with cute wire gate). Cross garden & exit via arch to road.

(8) Go R to A458. Go L & join old road for 200 yds (past cottage & bungalow) to take track L.

(9) Follow 400yds & join lane, which follow 1/2 mile to sharp R bend by farm.

(10) Take double gates ahead onto EARTH TRACK & cross stile R by gate. Cross field diagonally & take small gate onto track. Go L to its end & cross stile by gate

(11) Go to far R field corner & climb bank to cross stile. Follow R fence round wood to its far corner at stile R. DON'T CROSS.
FULL WALK - next para (12)

****

SHORT WALK
(11a) Put your back to stile, go ahead midfield & (when in view) head for brick thingys & cross stile. Follow R fence & cross stile. Follow L hedge to field corner water trough.

(11b) Go to R end of black shed & take gate. Go through farmyard & exit on track to sharp R bend.

(11c) Take R of 2 gateways, follow L hedge to field corner & cross 2nd stile BY GATE. Put your back to fence & go ahead midfield to middle of 3 oaks. Join grass track, then drive to road. Go R to start.
****

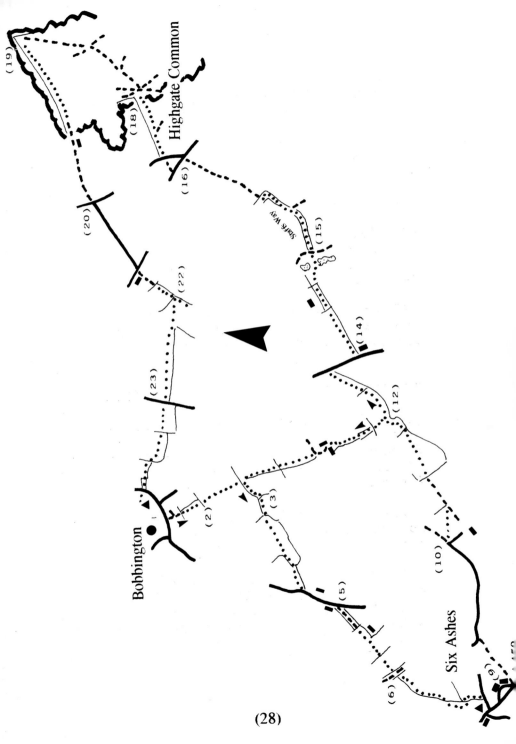

Bobbington

Highgate Common

Stiells Way

Six Ashes

(1) (2) (3) (5) (6) (9) (10) (12) (14) (15) (16) (18) (19) (20) (22) (23)

(28)

(12) Ignore stile & follow iron fence (via pond & gate) & take stile by gate to lane.

(13) Go R 200yds (past end of wood L & 1st gate L) to take 2nd gate L near farm (SW).

(14) Follow R hedge (via gates & through fenced section) to field. Go half R to pass between ponds, & via stile to track.

(15) Take gate opposite & follow fenced path (past gateway R & gap in L fence) then round L bend by wood to take gateway R. Follow earth track by R hedge to road. DON'T CROSS.

(16) Go L on verge 100yds & take entrance R. Pass buildings to road. Go L a few paces to brown gates & take fenced path on their R (SW)

(17) Follow 150yds to earth track with gateway L. Take path opposite & follow wood edge 300yds to wood corner.

(18) Take 2nd or 3rd path from R (they meet) & follow blue top posts & Staffs Way signs (where they part follow Staffs Way). Go on 1/2 mile to circular car park on corner of common. (New Lodge CP)

(19) Take path L past shed & follow wood edge 1/2 mile to meet track, which follow 1/2 mile to road.

(20) Take lane opposite 1/2 mile to road.

(21) Enter farm opposite & keep left to cross corner stile. Follow L hedge to field corner & take gate.

(22) Go half R to projecting hedge corner,
then go with hedge on your L 1/2 mile to lane.

(23) Go R 40 paces & enter field L. Cross
midfield to L side of cream bungalow & cross
hedge corner stile. Follow L hedge & cross
corner stile, then follow fenced path to road.
Cross stile opposite & take path back to start

Clent Hills Walks

WHERE ETC
These two walks start from the Visitor Centre in Nimm-
ings Car Park at the foot of Adams Hill. (Parking fee
currently 50p) The hills are signposted up a lane from the
A456 Birmingham - Kidderminster road. No buses.

Maps: Landranger 139, Pathfinders 933 SO 88/98 and 953
SO 87/97. Map reference SO 938808.

REFRESHMENTS
There is a refreshment kiosk at the Visitor Centre and we
note any pubs etc to be found on each walk.

THE HILLS & THE VIEWS
The Clents include Walton Hill at 315 metres to the east and
Adams Hill to the west at 304 metres. South from Walton Hill
is Calcutt Hill at 240 metres. They are part of chain of high
ground running across the southern edge of the West Midlands
from Kinver Edge to the Lickeys. The Clents have thin, stony
soil which supports woods and bracken on the slopes but only
heather and bilberry on the crests. Walton Hill is a big, round
dome with limited views, but from Adams Hill you can (sometimes) see The Wrekin, the Clee Hills, Radnor Forest and Hay
Bluff in Mid Wales, the Abberley Hills, the Malverns, and to
the south Breedon Hill and Edge Hill in Warwickshire.

Clent Hills, Hollies Hill & Calcot Hill

FURTHER REFRESHMENTS
Hill Tavern (Free House), Vine Inn (M&B), Four Winds
Restaurant and The Holly Bush (Free House).

HOW FAR
6 1/2 miles or a short walk of 5 1/2 miles.

THE HILLS, THE LEVEL AND THE ICE.
After the long shoulder of Adams Hill this walk descends
onto flat ground. A mile or so further on it climbs back up
Calcott Hill to follow one of the most glorious paths in the
Midlands before returning over Walton and Adams Hills.

The reason for the shapes of these hills and valleys emerges
at the top of Calcott Hill. Here you meet a boulder, which a
plaque tells you was carried by ice sheets from the Arenig
Mountain in North Wales. The Midlands was the meeting
point in the last (or latest) Ice Age of vast glaciers from
Wales, Scotland and the east. When they thawed some
10,000 years ago they dropped their gouged burden of
rock and sluiced billions of gallons of water across the
area to form these contours. The long hillside path that
follows crosses the top of a series of ice formed valleys.

*(1) Face front of Visitor Centre & take steps
L. Go R on track 1/2 mile to viewpoint.*

*(2) Go L to seat at foot of tree clump, then
head R down main slope. Keep to L side & pass
close by first & second pine clumps.*

*(3) Go on to draw level with pub, then cross
stile L. Go ahead, bearing R down steep slope.
Near bottom WATCH for & take small path SHARP
L, following it to stile & track.*

(4) Go R & climb to pass steps L, then curve L down to path junction by mark post. Turn sharp R & follow path down to road.

(5) Go R to cross roads. Turn L past church lychgate, then follow wall L up path to stile & field.

(6) Follow L hedge to its end, then bear R on clear path. Go through hedge gap to top field corner, & cross stile. Go ahead to track by National Trust sign.

(7) Go sharp R on track to meet lane. Go L 350 yds to just past Nursing Home & cross stile L.

(8) Go parallel with R hedge & pass farm to gate. Cross "stile" by it, then go half R to gate & cross stile to track junction.

****
SHORT WALK
Go L 3/4 mile to meet concrete track,
then switch to para (14).
****

(9) Take track opposite to L bend. Go just round it to gate R & cross stile. Follow R hedge to its corner, then keep ahead 125yds to draw level with projecting hedge corner R.

(10) Turn L parallel with road to cross footbridge. Keep same line towards double power poles & cross stile onto track.

(11) Go R 40yds to power pole & cross stile beneath. Go half L to road power pole & cross stile to A491.

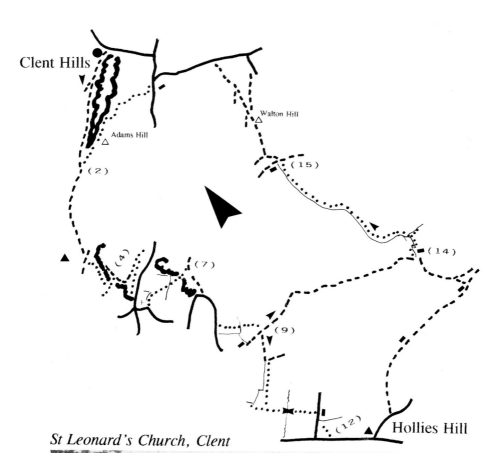

Clent Hills

Adams Hill

(2)

Walton Hill

(15)

(14)

(4)

(7)

(9)

(12)

Hollies Hill

St Leonard's Church, Clent

(33)

(12) Go L 300yds to pub & take Gorse Green Lane L. Follow it 150yds (past two entrances L) & take track L.

(13) Follow (passing R of barns) 1/2 mile to just past house L (Shut Coppice). Go L (via gate) to join concrete track, & follow it up to iron gates with track L.

(14) Cross stile by boulder. Follow R fence round R bend & cross stile. Go L & cross stile, then follow hillside path 3/4 mile to track by house L.

(15) Bear L between poles & take track curving R up to summit.

(16) Pass trig point & go ahead down ridge path to past seat R, then take any path L down to Walton Hill car park.

NEXT- Uffmoor Wood & Romsley walk para (22).

Clent Hills, Uffmoor Wood & Romsley

FURTHER REFRESHMENTS
The Fighting Cocks (Free House) at Romsley.

HOW FAR
6 miles

A CHURCH, A LEGEND AND A WOOD
This walk wanders to the west of the Clent Hills and starts with a long descent by a wooded stream. After a short excursion through a wood you follow level fieldpaths through grassland. The last section climbs Walton and Adams Hills.

St Kenelm's church and well are named after Kenelm, son of King Kenulph of Mercia who died in 821. A feud over the succession resulted in the little lad getting his head chopped off near here. There is a long yarn about how his corpse was unearthed, starring the Pope, a dove and an Anglo Saxon scroll, with walk on parts for an old lady and her cow. You can get the leaflet from the church. Suffice it to say that from the grave sprang a spring which would cure just about anything, so they built the church over it.

The nave and chancel of this small church are Norman, the tower and buttresses date from the late 1400's. The porch in small, rosy red bricks is Tudor. The gargoyles may have been carved as the usual cartoon faces, but are now eaten away by the weather and quite ghastly.

Uffmoor Wood was a "Harris Brush" wood. The Bromsgrove paint brush makers once owned 2,000 acres of woodland, but began to sell woods in the early 1980's. This one was bought by the Woodland Trust who invite you to wander as you wish. Older trees include the unusual whitebeam, bay willow and alder buckthorn, but most of the present trees are young. Harris's planted larch, scots pine, sycamore, alder, ash and poplar to grow small roundwood for brush handles, which has created an unusual and valuable habitat.

(1) From Visitor Centre, walk through car park to lane. Bear R & cross stile opposite.

(2) Go ahead past markpost & down to hedge corner to cross stile. Bear R (NOT AHEAD) & pass bushes on your R to markpost by hedge. Go R to its end, then bear L to cross stile.

(3) Go ahead (90 deg from stile & leaving R hedge) to take hedge gap. Keep same line to cross midfence stile.

(4) Go ahead into churchyard & meet tarmac path. Go L, pass church on your R & take small gate. Pass well on your R & cross stile.

(5) Follow fenced path & cross stile. Follow line of stream R (via stiles) for 1/2 mile, joining fenced path to track.

(6) Go R through gate to lane. Cross & take small gate into wood. Go ahead 25yds, then turn L & follow path parallel with lane. Cross grass ride with brick gizmo & continue to next ride. Go L to lane.

(7) Go R 350yds (past farm) & take track R. Follow it 300 yds to cross brick bridge, then cross stile R

(8) Go R to edge of wood & follow it 1/2 mile, crossing three stiles & steep valley. Continue R by wood to within 25yds of next hedge.

(9) Turn L & pass projecting hedge corner to cross stile R. Go ahead & cross next stile, then bear R up to midhedge oak & cross stile.

(10) Turn half L to cross stile, then half R to pass 30yds from midfield oak & meet track. Go L to gate & cross stile R.

(11) Bear R past pond to follow edge of wood & cross stile. Follow woodland path to cross next stile & climb steps to field.

(12) Go R by hedge (via two gates) to hedge corner with gate ahead & stile R. DON'T CROSS.

(13) Go L by hedge & cross corner stile to recreation ground. Go R into car park, then half L to cross corner stile onto road.

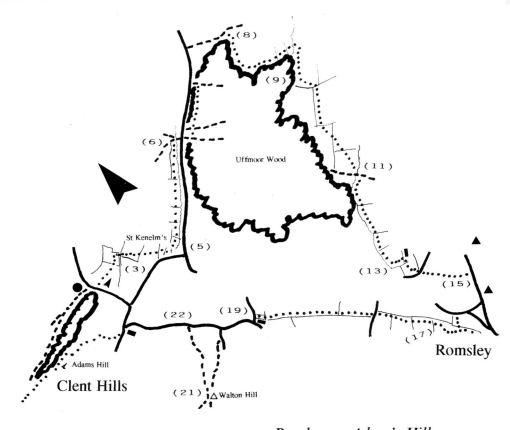

(8)

(9)

(6)

Uffmoor Wood

(11)

St Kenelm's

(5)

(3)

(13)

(15)

(22)

(19)

(17)

Romsley

Adams Hill

Clent Hills

(21) △ Walton Hill

Beeches on Adam's Hill

(14) Cross, go L past The Hedgerows & take tarmac path. Follow to join road, following that to T junction. Take tarmac path opposite & follow it over three roads to B4551.

(15) Go R 250yds to pass pub & take Poplar Lane R. Follow it 200 yds to timber railings L, & take kissing gate behind.

(16) Go up ahead to cross stile. Go R to hollow, bearing R past it & enter tunnel through bushes. Follow & cross stile to field.

(17) Follow R hedge 1/4 mile (via hedge gaps) to gate, & cross stile to lane.

(18) Go L few paces to gateway R & cross stile. Follow L hedge 1/2 mile (cross stile, pass stile L & take hedge gap) to cross stile by sheds, then go ahead to lane.

(19) Go L to junction & turn R. Follow lane 250yds to next junction.

(20) Go L 25yds to wooden stumps R. Take rising path behind up to summit trig point.

(21) Go R down ridge path to past seat R, then take any path L down to car park.

(22) Join lane & go L to T junction. Go L 100 yds & take path R. Follow rising main path (at fork go R) to summit.

(23) Pass four stones on your L & go down past R side of tree clump to view point with steel plaques. Take main track to start.

Kidderminster to Stourbridge

START, PARK & TRANSPORT
A one way walk from Kiddermister railway station to Stourbridge Junction station, with a short option starting from Blakedown. Get a bus to or park at Stourbridge Junction. Bus and train enquiries; 0121 200 2700.

Trains are normally quite frequent but: (1) MAKE SURE YOU GET ONE THAT STOPS AT KIDDERMINSTER (or Blakedown). (2) Sunday services are thin.

Maps: Landrangers 138 & 139, Pathfinders 933 SO 88/98 & 953 SO 87/97. Map references: Stourbridge Junction Station SO 910834, Kidderminster Station SO 838763.

REFRESHMENTS
There are pubs at both ends and at Blakedown but nothing between.

HOW FAR
9 1/4 miles or the short option of 5 miles.

JOURNEY THROUGH A SANDSCAPE
In that hazy, golden past when jolly red buses and single track railways doodled all over the country, chappies in long shorts with khaki rucksacks wrote walks from station to station. But with the decline of public transport almost the only linear walks now published are Long Distance Paths, like the Staffordshire Way. Circulars have a neat convenience, but they lack some indefinable excitement. A walk from, say Stourbridge to Bridgnorth is a journey, an adventure. This short adventure follows fieldpaths and long, straight tracks past pools, streams and pine woods, and has a general air of travelling somewhere.

Kidderminster is not far from the River Severn, so you start at the lowest point of the walk on a level of about 40 metres. The climb is very gentle, but by Blakedown you have reached 100 metres without knowing it, and when you meet the North Worcestershire Path at Hagley, you are at 140 metres. There is a slow decline to 100 metres at the end.

Alder trees dominate the waterside in the valleys and grew naturally, but the most common trees are various planted conifers which fill every patch of woodland. Most are Scots and Corsican pines, with some larch and Lawson cypress. However as you approach Blakedown watch out for some thin and lofty pines with smooth grey bark that look different. They are an unexpected (weedy) line of Douglas firs which have not yet developed the craggy red mature bark.

At the end of this walk you pass the fantastical tangle of tumbled and staggering tombstones in Old Swinford church-yard. We have tombs of sandstone, marble, slate and lime-stone built to every size from the simple headstone to gothic fantasies the size of garden sheds. Amongst the chest tombs a broken ionic column flutters with stone ribbon, there are plain crosses, wheel crosses, some with cog wheels for good-ness sake, Celtic crosses, pious angles, rudely plump half draped urns, stumpy Cleopatra's needles and an otherwise undescribable tapering cone topped by a feather duster. One luxurious resting place is supported by batteries of stumpy pink marble columns looking for all the world like hydraulic jacks. We need more of these.

```
(1)  From KIDDERMINSTER station exit to  A448.
Go  R 50yds, take Farfield R  & round  L  bend
(past Stewart Court) to A449.

*****************************************************
(1a)  From BLAKEDOWN station follow  Blakedown
etc  walk paras (1), (2) & (2a) - then  switch
to this walk para (15) and take it from *.
*****************************************************
```

(2) Cross, go R 250yds to house "Longhope" & take tarmac path L. Follow to lane & take gap opposite to golf course.

(3) Go ahead past L side of conifer clump to car park. Join tree lined track to green barrier & take path beyond to road.

(4) Go L 1/4 mile to roundabout on A448. Go R a few yds to bollard & cross. Go L to end of hedge then R to white house, & take track.

(5) Follow past sheds & across field to meet end of hedge. Track bends L; you go with hedge on your L & cross stile to nature reserve.

(6) Follow grass track & cross 2 stiles to long field. Head for farm, but just BEFORE gate go R down to field corner & cross stile to track.

(7) Go R 200yds (round L bend) to T junction of tracks. Go L 1/4 mile, pass Dunclent House to sharp R bend & take stile ahead by gate.

(8) Follow woodedge track 1/2 mile (past horse jumps) & take path down L.

(9) Follow 1/4 mile to junction of tracks at wood end. Go L & pass pylon to farm & road.

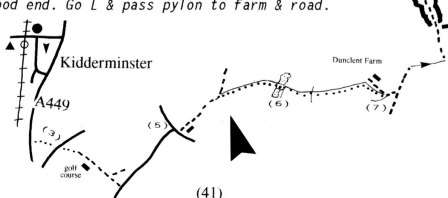

Kidderminster

A449

Mount Segg

Dunclent Farm

(12)

(11)

(9)

(6)

(7)

(3)

(5)

golf
course

(41)

(10) Go R 200yds past 1st stile L, cross bridge to gate, then take 2nd stile L. Go ahead & cross next stile to field.

(11) Follow L field edge 1/2 mile to meet fenced green track. Go ahead to ruin, bend L through dingle & join track to lane.

(12) Cross stile opposite. Bear R to cross midhedge stile. Keep same line over summit & cross field corner stile to track.

(13) Go L 1/2 mile to lane.

(14) Go R to L bend & take track ahead 1/2 mile to road.

(15) Take track opposite * 1/2 mile past house L to house ahead, then join drive to A456. VERY GREAT CARE.

(16) Cross, go R to house & take track L. Follow 1/4 mile to road.

(17) Go L & under railway, plus 50 yds to end of pool R, & cross stile. Follow fenced path to wood. Go ahead on woodedge path & join drive to meet end of lane.

(18) Go L & take wide track R of house. Follow by field edge, then between hedges, to lane. Go R 30yds & cross stile L.

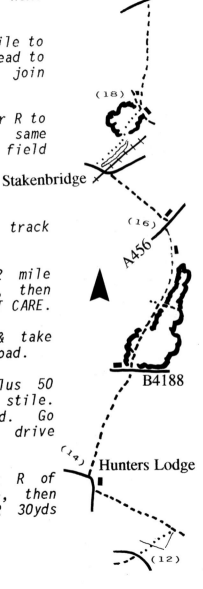

Stakenbridge

Hunters Lodge

(19) Follow L hedge to field corner, then follow path up past wood R & cross stile. Ignore stile R & follow R hedge to gate & track.

(20) Go R to T junction of tracks. Go L 1/4 mile, joining road to T junction.

(21) Take gap opposite, follow clear path over golf course, & join fenced path to road.

(22) Cross & enter sports field. Follow tarmac path & curve R between fences to road.

(23) Go L 150yds & take Swinford Rd R. Follow 1/4 mile to A491. GREAT CARE.

(24) Cross here, go R 100yds to house 205 & take path L. Go ahead (through iron gate, past church, over paths, through iron gate) & down under railway.

(25) Go L & take 1st path L to station car park.

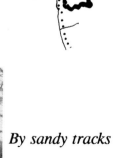

By sandy tracks

Kinver, the Wilderness & Castle Hill

WHERE
4 miles west of Stourbridge and best reached from the A449,
Kidderminster - Wolverhampton road. Maps: Landranger
138, Pathfinder 933 SO 88/98. Map reference SO 845834.

TRANSPORT, PARK & START
Buses call; enquiries 0121 200 2700. There are car parks
off the High Street. Starts from Ye Olde White Hart Inn.

REFRESHMENTS
George & Dragon (Ansells), The Vine (Free House), Olde
White Hart (Hansons), Plough and Harrow (Batham's),
several restaurants and a tea shop.

HOW FAR
About 7 miles

SANDSTONE & WOODLAND
A wander over the birch and oak woodland of Kinver Edge
and out into the remote country to the west. There are two
exhilarating ridge walks, a small, damp, interesting wood
and views over miles of hills and treetops.

Kinver is a sprawling village, but with the bulk of Kinver
Edge looming to the south and the River Stour and the Staffs
& Worcs Canal curling round to the east, it still has a focus
in the High Street. The river powered the village's industrial revolution between 1820 and 1870, when there were
five iron mills. From 1901 the Kinver Light Railway ran
to Amblecote near Stourbridge.

The huge, sandstone whale of Kinver Edge belongs to the
National Trust and Hereford and Worcester County Council.
From the crest are misty, blue views to the Clent Hills, The
Sheepwalks, the Clee Hills, Abberley Hills and Malverns.

Cave houses carved out of the red sandstone were quite common on the Edge; those at Holy Austin Rock were occupied in the Middle Ages by hermits. During the 19th century twelve families lived in such houses.

Half way round the walk you enter the 20 acre Widdow-sons Plantation. It is owned by the Woodland Trust, which aims to buy woods to preserve their amenity and conservation value. The Compton Brook trickles through, creating a wet valley in alkaline soil which is clay at the bottom but sand higher up, so offering a usefully mixed habitat. Tree species include ash, field maple, wild service tree, oak, hazel and crack willow. Smaller plants include bluebells, enchanter's nightshade, thin spoked wood sedge, stinking helebore and great hairy willow herb.

(1) Face Olde White Hart, go R past library & take Vicarage Drive L. At fork go R to Old Vicarage gate, then turn L down path to road.

(2) Go R 200yds to junction by postbox. Go L to speed sign, then R on drive to its end.

(3) Take path L of garage & follow it to take gate. Go ahead 50 paces, then R up steep, sandy path (via steps) to grassy shoulder. Go L up to crest.

(4) Go L on ridge path 300yds to where grassy spur veers L. Bear right past it, then take falling path R.

(5) Follow sunken track, curving R by low rock face & past paths L, to fork with oak in centre. Go L to next fork by overgrown seat L. Go R through horse barrier to path.

(6) Go L 1/2 mile on any paths, keeping parallel with lane R, to grass area with "No Riding" sign, & take gate R to lane.

(7) Cross to horse barrier opposite & take path. Follow through woodland, joining wood edge to fence corner, & take small gate to field. Go R by fence/hedge & cross stile to gorse patch. Follow R fence to stable & take gate R.

(8) CIRCLE round stable & take sunken path R into field. Go half L to hedge corner & take small gate. Go ahead 100yds to middle of field, then turn L to gate & road.

(9) Go L 50yds & take track R. Past R of black barn to approach house, then turn R to gate & take small gate. Follow grass track to join rising hillside terrace, & cross stile to field.

(10) Cross diagonally to pylon L (repeat - L) of midfield oak, & cross corner stile. Go down 50yds & cross stile R. Go ahead up bank to big fence post, then bear L by line of posts to stile & track.

Kinver

(2)

(4)

(5)

Kinver Edge

(9)

(7)

(12)

(10)

The Wilderness

(17)

(16)

(14)

(15)

(11) Go R 300yds to lane. Go L 200yds & take green track L.

(12) Follow via stiles & gates through wood to field. Go ahead by R fence (past gate R) & take gate ahead. Go up past L side of barn to field corner, & take 2nd gate L.

(13) Go R & take gate to track. Follow down to lane. Take track opposite & round R bend to house drive L. Go on 50 paces to end of conifer hedge & take path L.

(14) Follow hedged path (becomes track) 3/4 mile, then follow field edge to next corner & take green track L.

(15) Follow & take stile/gate. Go R across top of field & take stile/gate to track. Go ahead to house & take track L. Follow 1/2 mile & join lane to to road T junction.

(16) Take rising path opposite 200yds to horse barrier & wide sandy track. Go ahead up rising green ride (becomes path) up to horse barrier, & track junction.

(17) Go L 100yds to reservoir. Turn R & CIRCLE round it back to ridge path. Follow 1 1/4 miles back to topograph.

(18) Go R down cliff edge path down to grassy shoulder. Turn R down to crossroads of paths. Turn L & take gate & path to tarmac drive.

(19) Follow to road. Go L to junction. Go right 200yds to "Church View" L & take path just beyond. Follow to track & go R back to High Street.

Norton, Bunker's Hill & Iverley

WHERE
This walk starts from Mary Stevens Park, Stourbidge. Maps:
Landranger 139, Pathfinder 933 SO 88/98.

TRANSPORT & PARK
Buses pass; enquiries 0121 200 2700. Leave cars inside the
park near the gates on the town side, and start from here.

REFRESHMENTS
Apart from pubs in the town, The Greyhound (Banks's).

HOW FAR
About 7 1/2 miles or a short walk of 3 3/4 miles. Rather
muddy in places.

SMALL HILLS & SMALL WOODS
The landscape west of Stourbridge has many small hills
giving wide open views. It is part of the wide, sandy belt
which runs down the western side of the conurbation, and
woodland is unusually sparse. In the near distance are The
Million and Kinver Edge, but near the town there is little
but hedgerow trees, making the two small woods on this
walk especially welcome.

Norton Covert slopes steeply from the path on its west side,
falling about 50 metres to the road. Quarrying for sand has
left riotous contours of hills, hollows, ridges, bowls and
banks, which are clothed in beech, birch and oak, with some
sycamore and Scots pine. Bunkers Hill Wood was recently
acquired by the Woodland Trust (with some help from the
Stourbridge Ramblers' Group) and they invite you to wander
about at will. The trees are mainly well grown oak and
chestnut, but in one section there are Scots pine and larch
with a curious single row of western red cedar. These
conifers look like the familiar cypress, but note the red

bark and upright leading shoot. This wood demonstrates the live and natural growth of shrubs and flowers found beneath native broadleaved trees, and the dead, barren floor under the conifers. However, as you leave the wood you pass some lofty and handsome Scots pine, showing that some can be stately and attractive.

After Bunkers Hill Wood the landscape seems oddly bleak and deserted, with rough grass, reeds and straggles of hawthorn hedge. The reason is unromantic, for at one time this was part of a vast sewage farm where liquid waste was spread over the land in the hope that it would vanish, or something. Maps displaying the seductive contours of the small hills attracted walkers, who would be surprised by strange odours. Soon though, one of the odd little blue brick towers which dot the fields would explain matters with a gurgle. Dumping has long ceased, leaving you a rewarding walk with fine views in clean, fresh air.

Meet the North Worcestershire Path

(1) From park gates, go down main avenue past lake & playground to road. Cross into sports field, head for far R corner & exit to road.

(2) Go R to A451. Cross & go L 1/2 mile (past roundabout), to take Covert Lane R.

(3) Follow it to its end & enter wood. Follow woodland path & exit via horse barrier to track.   NEXT - para (4)

****
SHORT WALK
Go R 1/2 mile (across A451) to end of houses at track junction, then turn R.
switch to para (13).
****

(4) Go R 300yds (past end of road R) to road. Go L 250yds & pass Beechlands to cross stile R

(5) Follow hedged path into & through wood, & cross stile to field.

(6) Go ahead midfield to cross stile. Bear R & pass brick gizmo on your L to stile & road.

(7) Go L 1/2 mile & take concrete track L.

(8) Follow 1/2 mile to house & take gate ahead

(9) Follow R fence up to power lines, then bear L & take small gate. Follow L hedge & take small gate to track. Take small gate ahead & follow track through farm to lane.

(10) Go R a few paces, then bear L on track 300 yds to A451. DON'T CROSS YET. Go L 100yds to Staffs sign & cross to join fenced path R.

Stourbridge

Mary Stevens Park

(17)

(2)

A451

Norton

(3)

Norton Covert

(15)

resv'r

(13)

(5)

Bunker's Hill Wood

(7)

A451

(11)

(10)

(9)

(51)

(11) Follow 3/4 mile (past side paths & across lane) to triangular T junction with power pole

(12) Go L 1/2 mile to offset track junction with fat fencepost R, & turn R.

(13) Follow track 3/4 mile (past reservoir R) to T junction.

(14) Go L 1/4 mile, joining road to T junction

(15) Take gap opposite, follow clear path over golf course, & join fenced path to road.

(16) Cross & enter sports field. Follow tarmac path till it bends R, then bear L to L side of school, & exit to road.

(17) Go R to T junction. Go R round bend to T junction. Cross into park & return to start.

Stewponey & The Million

WHERE
Stewponey Bridge crosses the Staffs & Worcs Canal on the A458 Bridgnorth road at its junction with the A449 Kidderminster - Wolverhampton road. Maps: Landrangers 138 & 139, Pathfinder 933 SO 88/98. Map reference SO 861848.

TRANSPORT, PARK & START
Buses pass; enquiries 0121 200 2700 and 01785 223344. Park in and start from big layby by Stewponey Bridge.

REFRESHMENTS
The Stewponey (Banks's), The Cat (Free House) at Enville (closed on Sunday) and the Royal Exchange (Banks's) at Kinver.

HOW FAR
About 6 3/4 miles.

A CANAL, A FOREST AND A LONG TRAIL
With stretches of canal towpath, a woodland path and a long, wooded, sandy track between hedges, this circuit is a fair sample of the walking the area has to offer.

This section of the Staffs & Worcs Canal has two fairly straight reaches and two right angled bends as it leaves the Stour and continues north up the valley of the Smestow Brook. Swinging gently between mossy, sandstone cliffs and overhung with trees, it is lazily beautiful.

The vast and dense conifer wood that follows is for some reason called The Million. It was created after World War II on the site of an abandoned racecourse which was was once heathland. Most of the trees are Scots pines but there is some larch and Corsican pine. On the edges of the wood are oak, birch, alder, willow and sycamore. Neither Scots nor Corsican pines grow fast enough or big enough to be the most desirable timber trees, but on this dry, sandy site they do better than more most others.

You return to Kinver on the Staffordshire Way, which runs 93 miles from Mow Cop in the north of the county to Kinver Edge. It shows off the county's best landscape and many historic places including Congleton Edge, Rudyard Reservoir, the Caldon Canal, Churnet Valley, Shugborough, Cannock Chase, Brewood and Kinver Edge.

(1) From layby cross A458 to canal lock. Go upstream (not under road) 1 1/4 miles (past canal R) to Prestwood Bridge (No.34), and leave canal to join track.

(2) Go L 1/4 mile, crossing a lane & up to join lane.

(3) Go L (past farm and drives L) & join track ahead. Follow 1 1/4 miles (across several tracks) to gate & road. Take path opposite to bend of A458.

(4) DON'T CROSS - GREAT CARE. Go R on verge past house L, plus 100yds to gateway L, then cross & enter field.

(5) Go ahead past corner of wall & through fence gap. Go R with fence on your R to lane.

(6) Take path opposite & cross stile. Bear L to midfence jump & cross stile. Keep same line & take gate. Go R to drive & pool.

(7) Go L to R bend & take gateway ahead to join track. Follow 1/2 mile (past 3 R forks) to lane.

(8) Take gate opposite & continue 1/4 mile to bend of lane. CARE. Go R 100yds to junction & take path L.

(9) Follow 1/4 mile (via 2 stiles) to open field. Go ahead & cross stile, then follow fenced & tarmac paths to road.

(10) Go R to road. Take path opposite & cross 2nd road to bottom of 3rd. Turn sharp L on tarmac path & take road R (Church View Gardens).

(11) Follow 400yds past 4 roads L, & take 5th L (Foster Street) to main road.

(12) Go R 75yds round R bend & take drive L. Pass British Legion, then bear R past Community Centre to playing fields.

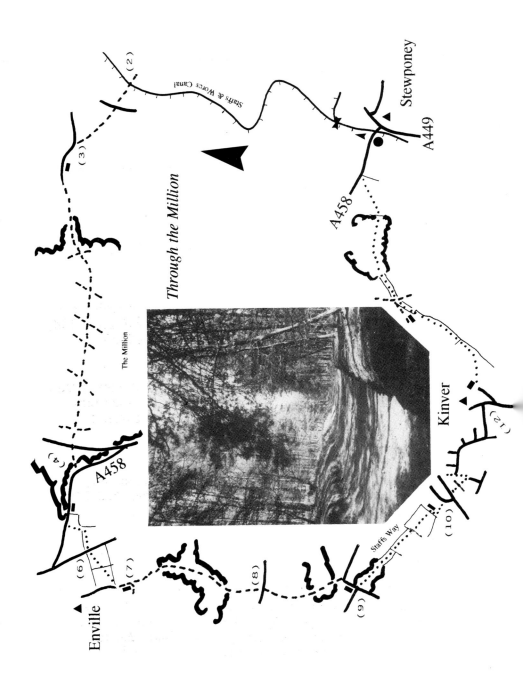

Through the Million

Staffs & Worcs Canal

Stewponey

A449

A458

The Million

Enville

A458

Kinver

Staffs Way

(2)
(3)
(4)
(6)
(7)
(8)
(9)
(10)
(11)
(12)

(13) Bear R & follow R hedge. Go ahead 1/2 mile, via gates & fenced paths, to track.

(14) Go L 15 paces & take fenced path R. Follow 1/2 mile through wood & cross stile to open field.

(15) Bear L to far L field corner & take small gate to A458. Go R down to start.

Two Canals & Two Rivers

WHERE
This walk starts from near the Cone at Wordsley, which is by the Stourbridge - Kingswinford road. Maps: Landranger 138, Pathfinder 933 SO 88/98. Map reference; SO 895865.

TRANSPORT, PARK & START
Buses pass; enquiries 0121 200 2700. Turn off the main road by the Cone and follow Bridge Street to its end, then turn left over the canal. Park cars near here and start from the green canalside area near "The Dock".

REFRESHMENTS
The Dock is an off licence, which is better than nothing. The Vine (Banks's) is near the start on the main road, and The Stewponey (Banks's) is beyond Stourton Bridge.

HOW FAR
About 6 3/4 miles.

TWO CANALS & TWO RIVERS
The walk starts at a canal dock and passes the famous Stuart Crystal Cone which once housed a glass furnace. You leave the urban area on the canal then join woodland and field paths. A second stretch of canal takes you through

some of our most beautiful waterside scenery before joining a sandy track leading back to the first canal.

The Stourbridge Canal starts from Delph Locks, about a mile above your starting point near the Cone, and runs only 5 1/2 miles to the Staffordshire & Worcestershire Canal at Stourton Junction. You will pass the Stourbridge Arm which curves towards the town centre. The contrast between the sections above and below the Arm is startling, dense Black Country industry giving way to serene countryside.

The "Staffs & Wuss" runs 46 miles between the Trent & Mersey Canal and the River Severn. You join it as it loops down the valley of the Swestow Brook and the River Stour. This was an early canal which followed contours to avoid changes of level, and hence the great cuttings and embankments of the later direct canals and the railways.

The third waterway on this walk is the River Stour, a hard-worked river which rises in the Clent Hills and drains the Black Country, then after a dozen rural miles has to accept the waste of Kidderminster before meeting the River Severn. As you walk down the Staffs & Worcs Canal you meet the Stour's main tributary, the Smestow Brook, which rises near Wolverhampton. Water quality in both rivers is poor, but they are valuable corridors for wildlife and support some fish, including gugeon, pike and dace in many places, eel roach and chub in some, and bream near Stourport. Even brown trout are seen in the Hoo Brook and sometimes where the Blakedown Brook meets the Stour.

(1) From The Dock, follow the canal downstream 3/4 mile (past branch canal, over river, past high fence R) & go under brick bridge.

(2) Take steps R, cross river & join track to T junction. Go L till track bends L, then curve R into wood. Follow wood edge path 17 paces & take rising path R.

(3) Go up to wood corner (ignore path L into field). Follow wood edge 1/4 mile, & after L bend go on 100yds to fork.

(4) Go R on main path (leaving wood edge) & by paling fence L to wood corner by field. Go L to cross stream and take barrier to drive. Go ahead to road and turn R to T junction.

(5) Go R 25yds to start of brick wall L, then cross & take gap into field. Follow R hedge to corner & cross offset stile.

(6) Go L a few paces into field & NOTE - 3 pylons. Head just left of middle one, & (when in view) head for gate, & cross stile to A449.

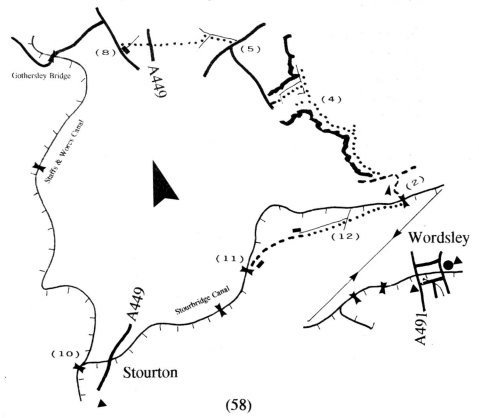

The Wheel Works at Cookley

Stourton Bridge

(7) Cross stile opposite, head for bottom R field corner & cross stile. Go L by fence to road.

(8) Go R 200yds & take lane L. Follow to canal & go L onto towpath.

(9) DON'T GO UNDER BRIDGE. Follow canal 1 3/4 miles to canal junction.

(10) Cross Stourton Bridge & follow towpath 3/4 miles (past locks) to brick bridge.

(11) Leave canal, cross bridge & turn L on track. Follow past farm & join path with hedge on your L, to stile & field.

(12) Bear L to meet canal at bridge. Cross & go R 3/4 miles to start.

Wolverley & Cookley

WHERE
3 1/2 miles north of Kidderminster off the B4189. Maps:
Landranger 138, Pathfinders 933, SO 88/98 and 953 SO
87/97 Map reference SO 829793.

TRANSPORT, PARK & START
Buses pass; enquiries 01905 763763. There are spaces
outside the Queen's Head pub, where the walk starts.

REFRESHMENTS
Queens Head (Banks), The Lock, (Banks) at Wolverley
and the Bulls Head (Banks) at Cookley.

HOW FAR
6 miles with a short walk of 3 3/4 miles.

SOME ARCHITECTURE, A RIVER & A CANAL.
A walk full of interest, with some odd buildings, two small
woods, the River Stour, the Staffs & Worcs Canal and a
mock castle.

Wolverley has some 17th century features but was built
mainly in the 18th or early 19th century. It has been des-
cribed as the village with the most personal character in
Worcestershire. The houses are mainly brick, some colour
washed in pinks, white and creams, and many have decor-
ative barge boards. The village is near a main road but feels
secluded in its sandstone hollow by the wooded valley where
the River Stour runs by the Canal. Cave cottages were cut
into the cliffs in the 19th century to house workers in the
iron factories.

The strange Jacobean building is the Court House, where
there used to be several law sessions each year. Two tiny

castellated turrets flank three pointed arches, supported by unneccessary buttresses, in front of perpendicular style windows. It was built in 1620 when they liked to lump architectural styles together. The red brick church of St John the Baptist scowls out over the village from a sandstone cliff. Built in 1772 to an Italianate design, it was remarkably forward looking, because it resembles a sadistic Victorian water works. It seems not to enjoy the delightful views across the wooded river valley and the village.

Here the Staffs & Worcs Canal is at its most beautiful as it meanders under wooded, sandstone cliffs. Compare it with the River Stour, which is glum-grey like a stressed out business executive racing to its meeting with the River Severn. The canal ambles by, all ambition spent and many years retired.

(1) Face Queens Head, go R 100yds to Gloster House R & take fence gap opposite. Follow L fence through woodland & cross stile to field.

(2) Follow R hedge & cross stile. Go half R to top L field corner, cross stile & reach lane. Go L 1/4 mile to farm, & just before it take tarmac drive R.

(3) Follow past gate ahead & cross stile R. Go L by fence (via stile) & cross stile to open field. Bear R (NOT AHEAD) to field CORNER, & take gap into wood.

(4) Go ahead by fence a few paces to track. Go L by fence & curve R 150yds to cross stile. Go ahead up to stile & lane.

(5) Go L 50yds & take lane R. Follow 1/4 mile to L bend, & cross corner stile R.

(6) Follow R fence 1/2 mile (round slight R bend) to sharp R bend, then keep ahead to projecting fence corner & cross stile.

(7) Follow valley to farm gate & cross stile. Go ahead to end of green shed, then circle right past farm. Follow track 25 yards & take track R. Follow (via gate & stile) to canal.

****
SHORT WALK
(7a) Go R 1 1/4mile to The Lock & B4184.
NEXT para (15)
****

(8) Go L 1/2 mile (via tunnel) to brick bridge, & cross it to join tarmac path.

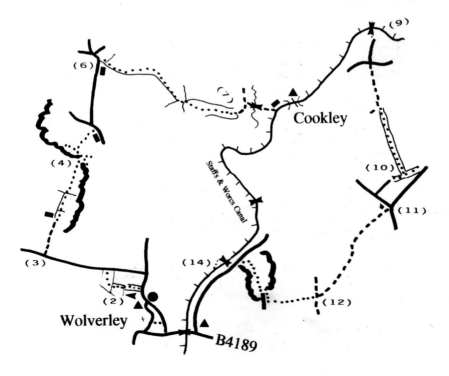

(9) Follow path & drive 200yds to lane. Take track opposite 300yds till it bends R, then keep ahead on hedged path (past exit R) to T junction.

(10) Go R & pass steel barriers to road. Keep ahead & join path to road. Cross, go L to road junction & enter castle gates.

(11) Go ahead, take small gate & join fenced track for 1/4 mile to track junction. Go L, curve past track L & on 1/4 mile to T junction by gateway R. Cross stile ahead

(12) NB 4 houses ahead; make for tree in middle of row & meet path. Go R & follow wooden fence round corner to its end. Follow path by fence through woodland to lane.

(13) Go L 150yds & cross bridge R. Bear L to join path & follow to canal.

(14) Follow 1/2 mile to The Lock & B4189.

(15) Go right through car park & take lane right. Follow 100 yards & cross two bridges, then take small gate left. Go up to church and join lane. Go right to start.

Drayton Pool (Belbroughton & Pepper Wood)